The Christmas Tree that Loved to Dance

A **Tall Tale** by

Miranda Hart

Illustrations by Lucy Claire Dunbar

MICHAEL JOSEPH

To Jill

The proof that perfect friendships
for certain seasons can be provided.

This is a story about a Christmas Tree that not only talks (yes, talks), but dances (yes you heard me, dances!); a dog called Jessie, who also talks; a woman called Joan, who – less surprisingly, in that she is a human being – talks too; two strange men (and yes, they talk) and their truck (which doesn't talk). There are also lots of lights and stars, and many a mishap. Interested? I should blooming well hope so! Right, I shall tell you all about it. Let's start at the start because it's usually best to start at the start rather than start at the end, don't you think?

Our tale begins in a rather ordinary way, with a fifty-five-year-old woman called Joan and her small ginger poodle, Jessie, walking around their neighbourhood for an evening stroll. Although when I say ordinary, I like to think that nothing is ever ordinary. If you see a woman walking her dog, you might think it normal, even a bit dull – but, actually, isn't everyone fascinating in their own way? Doesn't everything have a splash of the miraculous? I like to think so – you just have to look for it.

In this case, it turns out that this little woman's little walk with her little dog was anything but ordinary.

It was January in Leicester, England, United Kingdom, Planet Earth (just to be clear), so the evening walk was around four in the afternoon as it was already getting dark. It was a typical grey, shivery January day and Joan was shuffling along, quite keen to get back home and have a warm bath.

I don't want to worry you so early on in our story, but it was unusual for Joan to be shuffling. Being a joy-filled person, even in post-Christmas January, she was naturally more of a springy, even jumpy, kind of walker. But today, Joan was a shuffler. And a tripper-upperer – she shuffled around the corner, not noticing where she was going, and tripped up over a discarded Christmas tree before landing on some black bin bags. It was a soft landing but a very smelly one. A heady mix of bruised Brussels sprouts and curdling brandy butter. She would most definitely need that bath now.

Joan got up as quickly as possible to vigorously shake herself down. Watching this manoeuvre, Jessie thought it looked like she was shaking, in fact, much like a dog. Although not as effectively, as the vigorous shaky shake didn't dislodge a sticky yoghurt pot top that was stuck to Joan's bottom on her cosy padded coat. She peeled it off, looking around to check that no one had witnessed this awkward incident. Jessie was surprised by her beloved owner's reaction, knowing that in the past Joan would have got quite giggly at such a happening. It would be more like her to do something playful like run at the bins, leap high in the air – legs akimbo – and dive deliberately onto them again. But, you see, Joan was still mightily embarrassed by a few incidents that had happened before Christmas, many of which had made her look very peculiar (I can't wait to tell you one later). And so Joan really didn't want to be spotted at all, let alone in another seemingly strange way.

She shook off those memories, as well as the remaining scraps of rubbish on her coat (no one wants a mushy chestnut hanging off their person) and turned to continue her way back home. Suddenly, though, she heard a voice say, 'I am so, so sorry.'

This was confusing because nobody was around. Joan had just finished triple-checking. She wondered where on Planet Earth the voice was coming from. Was there someone hiding behind the postbox? No. Was somebody stuck up a tree? No. Was there anyone hanging out of their window? No. 'So sorry.' There it was again. 'It was my fault. I hope you are all right?'

Jessie started barking at the Christmas tree that was strewn on the pavement by the bin bags. Was Jessie telling Joan it was the Christmas tree speaking? Surely not? Joan cautiously approached, then quadruple-checked no one was around before daring to bend down towards the tree and whisper, 'Hello?'

'You tripped over me, and I just wanted to say sorry, oh dear, I really am so, so sorry.' Yes, indeed, the voice belonged to the tree. I know!

Now, some people might have screamed on hearing a Christmas tree speaking to them. Joan, however, was unfazed. She had discovered a few years earlier that she could understand Jessie's barking as if the poodle were speaking in English. One day, when Jessie was a puppy, Joan was pottering at home doing her chores when she heard a sweet, muffled voice say, 'I'm stuck, can you get me out?' She instinctively knew it was Jessie.

'Where are you?'

'In your wellie boot,' was the reply.

Sure enough she saw a furry bottom sticking out: Jessie was wedged right in. Joan giggled as she pulled her out. To anyone else Jessie the puppy was simply yapping, but Joan could hear Jessie's admonishment: 'Don't laugh, that was really quite scary, plus, I won't lie, your boots stink.'

Joan didn't question the fact that she and Jessie could suddenly communicate in this way. Indeed, she had once had a conversation with a sea turtle on holiday in the Caribbean, so nothing much surprised her any

more. I think there should be more people like Joan – accepting the miracles and mysteries of life.

'Are you okay? Please tell me you are okay. I am completely in the way. It's my fault – I am so sorry,' repeated the Christmas tree.

Joan was saddened to see that this lovely tree was lying discarded at an awkward angle – it couldn't be very nice. On a cold, grey pavement, in the damp January air, amongst rotting Christmas pudding, some old fairy lights in a tree nearby flickering and fading, and a once plump inflatable reindeer now flapping in the breeze. Joan was even more saddened that the tree was apologizing so much.

'Please don't worry,' said Joan. 'I am quite all right, no harm done.'

'She's fine,' reiterated Jessie – a bark to anybody else, but it turned out that the Christmas tree could also speak 'bark' like Joan. Perhaps because it was covered in bark. Who knows? There we are with another of life's mysteries.

'Still, you landed on the bins, and it was my fault for being in the way. I am so sorry . . .'

'Please, please stop apologizing,' said Joan. 'I was unusually absorbed in some silly worries and not looking where I was going. There's nothing for you to trouble yourself with, dear tree – you are not in the way.'

The tree looked surprised. Joan could see how much it wanted to believe her. But instead the tree could only repeat its earlier words, weepily now: 'But I am.'

'You're *not*,' said Jessie and Joan in unison.

'It all points to me being a burden.' The tree sobbed, 'There's no point to me; I am only making a mess.'

Joan knelt firmly down on the side of the pavement next to the tree to sort this out, and Jessie hopped onto her lap. Joan wanted to make sure this tree really understood what she was going to say.

'Now, listen to me. I don't see a burden, a mess, or something getting in the way. I see a beautiful, beautiful creation, that's all I see.'

'I agree,' said Jessie. 'I'll be completely honest with you: I very nearly weed on you but thought better of it as you smell so scrummy and piney.'

'Beautiful, did you say?' asked the tree.

'Yes,' replied Joan.

'No! No way. I think perhaps I was once, but not now, not lying here like this.'

Joan was very worried about this poor tree feeling so miserable. She was also aware that her legs were now extremely cold from sitting on the pavement and that Jessie had started shivering, so she knew they'd best go home.

'I tell you what,' Joan suggested, 'shall I prop you up against this big sycamore tree so you are at least standing and not lying on the pavement? That might make you feel a bit better.'

'Oh, yes, please. Thank you so much. And sor—'

'Shush, no more apologizing for you, please!' said Joan, kindly.

Joan hauled the Christmas tree up and leant it against the solid trunk of the sycamore that stood proudly in the street. 'You look lovely there,' said Joan.

'I don't think any of my friends will ever wee on you!' said Jessie.

Joan said goodbye to the tree, noticing what a gorgeous, unique shape it was, thick and round not only at the bottom but also in its middle, almost like one of those hedges you see clipped into balls, or a very large, neatly groomed poodle. Unlike Jessie, who was just a small ball of scruffy reddish fluff! Though that's exactly how Joan loved her.

As Joan lay back in her bath later, indulging in pine-scented bubbles in honour of her new tree friend (she had a collection of bath oils and creams to choose from), she mulled over something the tree had said. That it had felt beautiful in the past, but not now. A sinking feeling swept over Joan – perhaps the most vibrant and purposeful times in her life were behind her and she, too, was heading towards a different kind of season. Jessie, lying by the bath (and who indeed could have been mistaken for a bath mat), was sad to sense these thoughts from Joan, her most perfect, loving human.

Joan dipped herself under the warm water, and when she bobbed up she said a little prayer that her tree friend would feel better now that it was standing tall in a more natural way. She in turn felt better for helping another being feel better, and for now, that was enough.

The next day, Joan and Jessie decided to take their morning walk via the street where they had found their tree friend. Their usual routine was the opposite – park in the morning, street in the evening. And it was this fateful decision that ultimately led to their Big Adventure.

As they walked, Joan was amazed at quite how many Christmas trees were lying in clumps on various street corners. She knew this must happen every year, but now – after meeting Poodle Tree (her name for her new friend) – she was noticing it properly for the first time.

Jessie was too busy sniffing anything she bumped into to listen to Joan's observation. That's the thing with dogs – unless you sit them down, look them straight in the eye and get them to fully concentrate, they will flit from sticking their head in a paper bag to chasing a seagull to sniffing a wall to meeting another dog and deciding whether to play with it or just sniff its bottom and move on.

Joan may have also noticed the strewn trees in a fresh way because, for the last few years – despite absolutely adoring Christmas trees – she hadn't had one in her house. Joan had been spending Christmas in St Winnifred's Care Home, where her mother resided. This year was the first that Joan had had at home in a long time. It was bittersweet without her mother, but she'd bravely found joyful, delicious moments to savour about her favourite season – reading by the fire, different-smelling bath salts every night, playing games . . . Jessie's favourite was Jenga. Which meant Joan building the tower and Jessie running full pelt at it to knock it over. And repeat! Joan's favourite game was a ridiculous one she'd invented – flick the bread sauce on the donkey!

The aim of the game was to throw a lump of bread sauce, blindfolded, to land on the face of a hanging picture of a donkey. Absolute carnage. Joan didn't even like bread sauce, but nonetheless made it for the Christmas ritual. And it never failed to make her laugh. (Jessie, meanwhile, loved hoovering up any bread sauce blobs that missed the picture or plopped slowly off the walls. As I say, absolute carnage!) But, having been out of the habit of Christmas at home, and her mind on other things, Joan had missed out on getting a tree and decorations this year.

Joan thought how incredibly sad it was to see all these Christmas trees thrown onto the dreary, damp pavements. Once the colourful, beautiful focus of a warm room, now simply neglected after the festivities. They looked so undignified and uncomfortable. And then Joan was struck by some very, very important thoughts indeed: *Where do they all go? Are they thrown out with the other rubbish to join landfills?*

Do they get chopped up and sold for wood to burn?
Or just go from being a splendid composition in
someone's home to disgustingly decomposing into
smelly compost? Joan became most perturbed. And
even more so when she turned the corner onto the
street where she and Jessie had found Poodle Tree
last night: two men she had never seen before were
sloppily throwing some other Christmas trees into the
back of their truck. They weren't the rubbish clearers
Joan knew, or the tree surgeons who expertly pruned
large trees like the sycamore. Their truck wasn't
labelled, and she felt sure any respectable company
would have a professional name displayed (she knew
the local dog groomers – Short, Bark and Sides – had
recently had a wonderful new sign painted on their

van; and let's please acknowledge the utter joy of that name). Joan felt it was her duty to approach them, to make sure all was above board and hopefully get some answers. She marched up quickly, noticing their scruffy boots, caps and dismal grey-black boiler suits, one of which was so ill-fitting that the crotch of the trousers section was almost dragging on the floor.

'Excuse me . . .'

On seeing her, the two men guiltily leapt into the front of the truck, stumbling over their clodhopping boots, such was their rush, and quickly started the engine.

'Hey, wait!' shouted Joan, trying to stop them. But they ignored her and thundered down the road at high speed, almost taking off upon hitting a speed bump. Jessie was barking furiously. Joan agreed as she interpreted the barks – those two men looked like they were up to something. They seemed very suspicious indeed. If nothing else, it was their beards.

I should add that I'm not saying there is anything wrong in a beard. Beards can look mighty fine on many people. I know one man who combs his long beard every hour, he's so proud of it. He likewise has a moustache that manages to stick out like a walrus and it's magnificent.

I also know a woman who started growing beard
hairs when she was seventy, decided to let nature
take its course and now has a gorgeous, fluffy, white-
haired chin – her friends lovingly call her Mrs Santa!
So, beards can certainly be funny and fantastic things.
But those particular beards on the men in the truck,
well, they struck Joan and Jessie as very odd indeed.

Joan and Jessie hurried along to check on Poodle
Tree. They were mightily relieved when they saw
she was still there leaning against Sycamore, and
smiled when they saw a star had been placed on top
of her, giving her a rightful noble status (apparently
a passing child had seen a dropped one and asked
her father to lift her up to place it on Poodle Tree's
top branch). Not only that – the two trees
were having a delightful conversation,
comparing notes on what it was like
to have needles instead of big, lobed
leaves, and Poodle Tree was really
interested to know what it felt like
for Sycamore to lose his luscious
lobed leaves in winter.

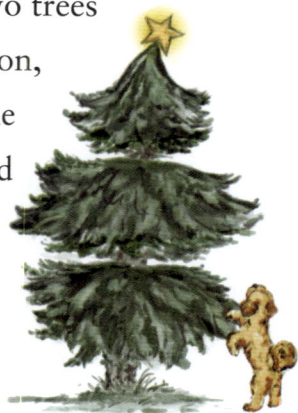

Joan and Jessie listened with much intrigue as Sycamore reassured Poodle Tree that he didn't feel cold, but he did sometimes wish people would appreciate him as much in the winter as they did in the summer.

Everything seemed happy on this little street corner, and Joan and Jessie, swept up in the fascination of a chat between two trees, had momentarily forgotten about the strange men until an unnerving rumbling sound interrupted their thoughts, and indeed spooked them all. It was a deep *thud, thud* noise. They looked around, almost expecting to see a dinosaur plodding down the street – it felt like the noise shook the ground. It turned out it was a disturbing sort

of dance music, and it was coming violently and
excruciatingly loudly from the very same truck they
had seen minutes before. Joan and Jessie hid with
Poodle Tree behind Sycamore to spy on the
bearded men.

Now, forgive me for digressing again for a very brief
moment, but I also wish to add that I am not saying
there is anything wrong with dance music as such.
Not at all. Music always lifts the spirits, don't you
think? In fact, Joan loved music and had been a very
keen dancer in her youth (her natural springiness
made her particularly good at the jive). Sadly she gave
it up when it seemed her friends were only there in
the hope of finding romance. Joan didn't mind who

she danced with – taller, shorter, male, female – as long as they loved dancing. She just wanted to dance for the sheer joy of it. And to all kinds of music – she'd done a belly dance to Bollywood and the Calypso in the Caribbean. But this *thud, thud* type of music – well, Joan thought it was simply a horrid thump that had no musicality to it whatsoever and was intrusive to the beauty of life's natural noise. Don't you just love birdsong and the rustling of leaves? This sounded as mean as the mean-looking men in their mean truck who were meanly intruding on this lovely street and, in this case, stealing innocent Christmas trees.

Joan and Jessie peered around Sycamore and could
see that the men were themselves peering around
to make sure that no one was looking. They then
grabbed two more Christmas trees, slamming them
down in the back of their truck. Small sprigs of
branches were dropping off the trees, they were

so badly handled, and remaining pieces of tinsel and shards from a broken bauble scattered the street. It was all too wretched to see. And rather moving, for Joan and Jessie had become aware of the trees humming to one another to keep their spirits up.

'Hide me,' whispered Poodle Tree, terrified she might be discovered and driven away in such a fashion.

Joan opened her coat as wide as possible and covered up Poodle Tree. Luckily the men didn't see them and instead sped off into the distance. Jessie barked after them then quickly grabbed the remains of a sandwich out of a bin before Joan could stop her.

Joan was distracted on realizing that she had remained leaning against her Christmas tree friend with her coat wide open, revealing her bobbly reindeer jumper and the leggings she normally only wore around the house. It would have amused her, but unluckily Daniel, the man who owned the dry cleaner's and tailor's at the end of Joan's road, happened to turn onto the street. Daniel was shy but polite and charming, and his kindly smile suddenly changed to curiosity as he peered at Joan in her bizarre stance. For some reason, Daniel *always* seemed to find her in strange situations.

Instead of confidently saying hello to Daniel, Joan awkwardly tried to cover up her 'odd open coat to hide Poodle Tree' pose. For some unknown reason, she thought the answer was to pretend she had been dancing, opening and closing her coat and then shimmying her back against the tree.

Jessie covered her eye with a paw in embarrassment – it looked like Joan was either trying to flash her leggings or, even more bizarrely, scratch an itchy back like a bear in the wild. Daniel walked on, quickly, breaking into a trot, probably a little afraid!

Before Joan could wallow in her embarrassment, let alone compose herself, she noticed that Poodle Tree was shaking and dropping needles. 'I hope those men won't throw me in their truck. Where are they taking all my friends? I'm scared,' said Poodle Tree.

Joan and Jessie paused. Then they looked at each other. It was a look they had shared before. A look of, *Right, I'm going to do something about this,*

I have to help. Joan found herself saluting Jessie. With such a sense of purpose, the fear of what Daniel thought of her, or anyone else for that matter, suddenly evaporated. Joan told Poodle Tree she would go home and get out of her job for the day – and be back as soon as she could to help. She was absolutely *not* going to let Poodle Tree be captured.

Joan and Jessie marched briskly home, doing what they called their 'we're on a mission walk', singing, 'Off to embrace a mission, a wonderful J and J mission,' to the tune of 'We're Off to See the Wizard' from *The Wizard of Oz*.

At home, Joan rang the primary school where she taught art and music to say there was an emergency. She promised the headmistress it was important. Little did the headmistress know that in this case the 'emergency' was actually a Christmas tree shaped like a groomed poodle. And, in fact, not just Poodle Tree. Joan being Joan had decided she was going to help all the trees she had seen collapsed on her street during these bleak January days and nights. She couldn't sleep soundly on her soft mattress next to a sweet-smelling cardamom candle, knowing the trees were lying on a cold hard surface with the smell of a putrid pig-in-a-blanket.

Joan thought again about how sad it was that these trees had only recently been adorned and adored over Christmas, with lights and sparkles and baubles. They were the centre of a person's sitting room or kitchen or hallway, making a home jolly and safe and beautiful. Presents would have been placed lovingly underneath them and they would have been crowned with stars or angels or in some cases Santa hats, and in one case – rather unusually – a cowboy hat. Either way, they were treated royally, which was quite right for all they offered. Then came the first week in January and what did people do? They dismantled their finery and threw their trees out onto the street, not even saying goodbye or thinking about where they might end up. (Joan felt a fraction ashamed that she might have been guilty of this, too, in the past.) All that people seemed to care about was that the trees were cleared away by someone else and not cluttering up their hallways. Joan wondered if anyone even noticed them as they rushed about their day, frowning with their heads down, the Yuletide jolly human spirit seemingly as discarded as the trees.

Joan was actually feeling quite angry about it all. And that was no bad thing – anger about an unfairness can show you care, and it gave Joan the energy to move some furniture in her house and clear away lots of her belongings. You see, she was making space and Jessie knew exactly why. Being a dog, Jessie couldn't lift furniture or move books, so her job was to simply sit on an armchair looking beautiful. And that was a job she believed she did very well indeed! But she was excited for what was going to happen next. And sure enough, after a few hours of organizing, off they went outside.

Here's the thing – Joan's plan was to bring the trees back into her house before they were stolen by the bearded men, keeping them warm and safe until she could figure out what to do with them. Joan was going to go straight to Poodle Tree, but then she saw a miserable clump of trees lying on the corner opposite her house and couldn't help but quickly rescue them.

As she strode purposefully over to the trees, her spring very much back in her step, they started quivering. Joan was attuned to this and whispered, 'Don't worry, I'm here to help,' and (gently) dragged the one on the top of the pile over to her house before propping it up in her sitting room. Joan went to rescue the next tree. And the next. She ignored the soil, wood and pine needles on the floor – now was not the time for tidiness. Luckily most people were at work, and the street was nicely quiet. Almost eerily so in this post-Christmas haze. But guess who was the one person who saw her dragging a tree into her house? Yes, of course, it was Daniel. Joan waited with dread for an inevitable comment. Instead, without any fuss, he kindly asked, 'Would you like some help?'

Joan was surprised. 'Oh yes, that would be lovely, thank you.' Her arms were quite sore by now, as this was the sixth tree she had moved. Daniel picked up the other end to carry it with her, but as soon as Joan started taking it into her house, Daniel stopped moving. 'Are you taking this Christmas tree back inside?'

Joan suddenly realized how it looked. Daniel had probably thought she was simply moving the tree out of the way.

'Umm . . . well, yes, I am . . .' said Joan, knowing she couldn't lie at this point – she was nearly at the front door.

'Why?' asked Daniel.

'Ummm . . . well . . . you see . . . ummm . . .'

'Say something, ANYTHING,' barked Jessie.

'I just LOVE Christmas!' shrieked Joan. 'I miss it SO MUCH!'

'But it was only a couple of weeks ago,' said Daniel, putting one finger in his ear for Joan's shriek was almost deafening!

'I know. I just can't bear the fact it's over for another year, and January and February can be such awful months so I thought I would get a tree and have Christmas for a bit longer.'

'I see. Well, I think I see . . .' mumbled Daniel.

Then Joan heard Jessie barking madly at the front door. She was telling her she couldn't let Daniel come in with the tree because there were five others in there already! What would he think if he saw her sitting room full of other people's old Christmas trees?

'I can take it from here,' said Joan quickly.

'Don't worry, not much further,' replied Daniel.

Joan was beginning to sweat with worry now, so she shouted in a fluster, 'Please just leave this to me, it's a deeply private matter!'

She shouted so loudly that Daniel jumped and
dropped the end of the tree he was carrying.

'I have very particular rituals around Christmas and trees and things, you see!' she said, still shouting for a reason she could not fathom but probably due to panic. Jessie's paw was once again over her face in embarrassment.

'I will leave you to it.' Daniel gave her a nervy, wide-eyed stare, clearly confused, before he backed away. He walked backwards, staring at Joan for quite a long time (like you might do when leaving the room of a king or queen), before turning. Perhaps worried she might do something to him. 'That could not have gone any worse unless you had bent down and ripped your trousers in front of his face,' said Jessie, giggling. 'Oh, do shush,' Joan grumbled.

Joan and Jessie now had six Christmas trees
in the sitting room and – despite what Daniel
clearly thought of them – were feeling pleased
with themselves. Jessie was even more pleased by
something appearing from her owner she had very
much missed of late – a smile. The trees looked so
much happier being upright and inside in the warmth.
Joan thought she heard one of them whisper, 'Thank
you,' though they were likely too shaken up and
tired to spark conversation, bless them. Joan too was
feeling tired and was about to pop the kettle on when
Jessie reminded her they had to get Poodle Tree.
Off they marched once more, humming to keep up
their morale, as they'd heard the trees do earlier.

On her way out, before shutting the front door, Joan called out, 'Don't worry, won't be long,' to her new tree friends. And at that precise moment, Nellie, the next-door neighbour, walked out of her front door.

'Oh, have you got friends to stay?' Nellie asked.

'No,' said Joan. 'Oh, I see, yes, sort of . . . yes . . .'

'Oh, like that, is it? Well, I don't want to pry . . . Not being a nosey neighbour, but lucky you . . . Have fun, wink.'

Oh dear. Not only did Daniel think Joan was
completely absurd, shouting at him about her January
Christmas tree rituals, but now her neighbour
thought she had a romantic fancy man staying when
it was actually six pine trees. What a muddle! In fact,
you could say everyone was barking up the wrong
tree . . .

Joan and Jessie were walking to the street Poodle Tree
was waiting for them on when they were stopped in
their tracks by a distant thud of music. Oh no! Were
they too late? They started running, Joan leaping
unnecessarily highly over the Christmas trees and bin
bags lest she tripped again, and as they frantically
turned the corner, the worst thing was happening

– they could see Poodle Tree being thrown into the truck by the men with their long, unkempt beards. One beard was so ropey and dangling it got caught on a lamppost and spun one of the men around, whilst the other briefly scooped up a passing cat in his baggy crotch. If they weren't so sinister, Joan might have thought they were party clowns. Joan and Jessie raced towards Poodle Tree. They could hear her cries.

'Help, help, where are they taking me? Oh no. I bet this is because I was in the way and tripped you up . . . Help!!'

'Wait, stop!' screamed Joan to the men. 'Who are you, and what are you doing with the trees?' But, as before, they hurtled into their truck and sped away, caps lowered, loud music blaring, drowning Joan out. Joan and Jessie stood in the middle of the street, defeated, with only Poodle Tree's star lying crumpled in front of them. Such a sorry sight to see Poodle Tree's crown knocked off her head. Joan felt a sinking feeling again – having had the very new privilege of talking to trees (she had thought it would only ever be a sea turtle and a dog – oh, and a crow that one time), she felt heartbroken watching her new friend disappear into the distance, right in front of her eyes.

A calm, loving voice spoke out: 'Lean on me.' It was Sycamore. And that was just what Joan needed. A strong, kindly being to sink into and help with her disappointment. She leant against Sycamore and breathed a big sigh as Jessie nestled her little bottom against Sycamore's comforting, solid trunk.

'Where do they go, do you think?' Joan asked Sycamore.

'I don't know. I can't imagine what it must be like, to be uprooted like that. I have always known that this is my forever home, and my roots grow stronger every day right here. To be suddenly chopped down or moved around – it is a horrible thought.'

'But they offer such a gift to us all at Christmas, don't they? Twinkling and sparkling in our homes?' said Joan.

'Very true, very true,' replied Sycamore. 'I wouldn't fit in a house and would make a terrible mess. It must be very special for people to have a tree in their house in winter.'

'And the trees are so patient to let everyone cover them in decorations,' said Jessie. 'I'm never happy if someone tries to put me in clothes – it's very uncomfortable and frankly humiliating.'

'But that's the thing,' said Joan pensively. 'I think they love it. Poodle Tree adored having her star back on in the street. They are so kind to sacrifice themselves for a short season knowing how much joy it brings.' Joan wished she had given one the opportunity to do just that and shine with purpose in her home. Her sinking feeling was stirring in a different direction. Don't worry, not heartburn, but the energized call to action was returning. Since Joan couldn't save Poodle Tree right at this moment – though part of her stirring was to do just that – she decided to keep saving as many of Poodle Tree's friends on the local streets as she could. *No one,* thought Joan, *should feel discarded.*

For the next two days and the next two nights, Joan and Jessie worked tirelessly on their mission, taking trees back to their house. It was hard work for Joan (Jessie was the best cheerleader she could possibly be, but the heavy lifting was all Joan's), and there were a few tricky moments when she nearly got caught.

For instance, early one morning before the sun had come up, the local baker was approaching on his way to work, so Joan quickly lay down on the pavement and put the tree she was carrying on top of her to hide. She lay there as still as she could, not wanting to be discovered lying underneath it, with Jessie

snuggling tightly in her armpit. Luckily the only
thing that found them was a neighbourhood fox. I say
luckily . . . It wasn't that lucky when the fox sniffed
about in places Joan most certainly did not want to
be sniffed in! The less said about that the better.

The next moment wasn't much better. As Joan started to move out from under the tree, a rather proper woman she knew from flower-arranging at church was starting one of her 'early-morning constitutionals', as she called them. 'Joan, is that you?' asked the posh woman. 'No, it's not me, it's not Joan,' said Joan. Which obviously didn't work as an excuse because it was clearly Joan's voice and indeed clearly Joan's face talking to the woman she clearly knew. Exclaiming you aren't who you are when you are who you are is never going to get you out of a tricky situation!

'What on earth are you doing lying underneath a Christmas tree?'

'Am I?' said Joan, deciding that acting as if she didn't know what had happened might excuse her strange behaviour. 'How odd! Silly me!'

'I think it's best you go home and have a stiff cup of coffee, Joan,' said the woman sternly.

Joan realized that the posh woman, who she had always been slightly scared of, thought she was inebriated and that was why she was lying on the pavement and needed a cup of coffee to sober up. Joan went along with this, thinking it was probably easier than explaining her mission, and so sang, pretending to be completely and utterly sozzled. She kicked her legs in the air, doing the hokey-cokey with the tree, as the woman speed-walked away, shaking her head and tutting disapprovingly. Jessie had hid under a car and put her head in a discarded crisp packet, unable to watch.

And then there was the moment, in the light of the early afternoon, when Joan had got quite a big tree wedged into her front door. She was pushing it in, with much huffing and puffing (from both Joan and

the tree, and Jessie for empathy), and while the trunk was still firmly sticking out her neighbour appeared. Joan was screeching, 'Get in, you, come on, you can do it, get inside!'

'But I am going out,' said Nellie. 'I don't want to go inside.'

'What? Oh, I see . . . I wasn't talking to you,' said Joan, who quickly stood in front of the tree trunk to hide it from Nellie.

'Oh, is that your fancy man?'

'Umm . . . yes . . .'

'Here we go,' muttered Jessie to herself, knowing that the odds with this mission was it was going to lead Joan to yet another muddle.

'Ooooh, but I must meet him . . .' said Nellie nosily.

'No, he's very shy – get inside, you!' She pushed the tree harder. 'He's rather fat, you see, needs a good shove!'

'Ow, that hurt, your silly prickles!' said Joan before she realized what she had said.

'He has PRICKLES?!' exclaimed Nellie.

Then with an almighty shove, Joan pushed the tree through the door and went flying in with it, landing on top.

'Oh, well,' Nellie said naughtily, 'you are obviously both getting on very well.' Joan quickly leapt up and pulled the door ajar. 'It's not what it looks like!' she yelled. Just to cap off this sequence of awkward events, Daniel – yes, of course, Daniel – walked past carrying his shopping.

'Coo-ee, Daniel, guess what – Joan seems to have a fancy man . . . not that I'm being nosey . . .' said Nellie. (May I add – saying 'I'm not being nosey' when you are being nosey doesn't make you not nosey!)

'A fancy man?' asked Daniel. 'Oh. Really?'

'Acting like teenagers if you ask me. Apparently, he has prickles, but I really don't think we should ask any more about that!' said Nellie. 'Let's leave them to it – bye-bye, you two!'

Oh dear, oh dear. This mission was giving Joan the strangest reputation. And that is saying something, after the bigger incident that happened before Christmas. I will pause our story briefly to tell you, as I promised I would. Plus, I can't wait any longer.

You see, a few weeks before Christmas Joan volunteered to take some of the elderly occupants of St Winnifred's Care Home to a local nature reserve for a day out. She hadn't been there for a few months since her mother had died and was missing the group she had got to know from her regular visits. In many ways, they'd become her closest friends. Joan knew that a few of them were avid observers of – and very knowledgeable about – the many birds that visited the feeders that hung around St Winnifred's well-tended gardens. They often watched them together – Joan organizing their chairs so they could sit in a row along the French windows, playing a live version of Bird Bingo. Joan would get giggly as they got more and more rowdy shouting 'Robin' or 'Chaffinch' or slightly harder when said quickly 'Great Spotted Woodpecker' to be the first to say the names!

So her generous suggestion of taking a few of them to the local RSPB nature reserve for a day's birdwatching was extremely well received. Fresh air, a change of scene, a little bit of exercise, a cake in the café – what could go wrong?

Well . . . it was all going swimmingly as they wandered happily between the bird hides, linked by elegant pontoon walkways, looking at the winter migrants on the lake. Then, when in one of the larger wooden bird hides, Joan leant forward to grab her Thermos flask off the floor for a cup of tea she startled herself by – inadvertently – breaking wind. Very loudly. In the cavernous hide, the noise of said emission took on a deep and sonorous timbre. She was glad she didn't have any tea in her mouth for she would have spat it out for laughing, especially as she was sure she heard her wind noise echo back at her. But before she could laugh with the others or utter an apology, one of the elderly men had excitedly identified the sound as the 'boom' of the bittern – a rare type of heron whose plumage blends in so well with the reed beds that it is virtually invisible and very difficult to spot.

They had all come alive with the excitement and Joan couldn't bear to contradict their findings and thought that the episode could safely be left behind (as it were).

Alas the tale took an unfortunate turn when, after
excitable word had spread, the local newspaper ran a
story about the return of the bittern to the area after
an absence of nearly a hundred years. Joan couldn't
let this go unchecked – people might decide to come
from far and wide to see said bittern, when it was
just an explosion from her bottom. Joan wrote to the
editor explaining the whole thing. She apologized
for all the palaver it had caused and asked that they
set the record straight with a short retraction.

The newspaper did duly set the record straight. Unfortunately, they did so by exposing the whole incident with Joan's picture and titling the article 'BITTERN ON THE BOTTOM'.

It was the talk (and giggles) of the town for more than a few days. As well as many disappointed mumbles and grumbles amongst keen ornithologists (not to be confused with orthodontists – Jessie wondered why dentists were so upset by the lack of a rare bird!). It was no wonder Joan wanted to keep a low profile. Dear Joan, she had only been trying to do a good thing.

Joan had hoped all the attention and embarrassment was behind her, but with her recent tree-saving mission, people now thought she was either drunk, rubbing a scratchy back like a bear, weirdly obsessed by Christmas or having a passionate love affair with a very large prickly man. But despite all, Joan felt the mission was justified. She had now saved a whopping thirty-three trees. Joan could barely move in her house – there were Christmas trees *everywhere*. In her sitting room, it was trees, trees, trees. There were at least eight trees surrounding her bed. Five or six in the kitchen and even a couple in the bath. Her house was basically a pine forest. It reminded her of the thick and beautiful Black Forest that she had trekked through when she was younger.

Joan and Jessie spent a lovely couple of days hiding
at home with their tree friends. They had found
some Christmas decorations in the shops going very
cheaply as, of course, the season was over. But not
for Joan and Jessie it wasn't. It was full-on Christmas
again in a way that no one had ever done Christmas

before – I don't think anyone has decorated a tree and popped it in their bath! Not even the king has had thirty-three trees, though there *would* be room for a forest inside Buckingham Palace.

And now each of Joan's trees had lights and a star on top, baubles, tinsel – all fully splendid and dignified. In turn, Joan was much cheerier than she had been in a while as she continued the Christmas spirit she loved so much. She was generally dinging and donging merrily on high all over the place!

Now, I'm all for singing and creating jollity, especially during dark winter months. I've even been known to do a quick round of 'Jingle Bells' in June to boost my

mood. But it's time to buckle in because I'm afraid that this tale is about to have a lot less harking of the herald angels singing, resting of the merry gentlemen, good old King Wenceslas wenceslasing or any fa-la-la-la-la-ing. Instead, it's about to become much more of a very bleak midwinter. I know this might be troubling to hear, so I won't delay any longer in telling you what happened.

To begin with, Joan and Jessie were finding their post-Christmas forest quite fun and cosy. On the evening that they finally got all thirty-three trees connected to the power supply for their fairy lights, they prepared a little ceremony to switch on said lights and show the trees in all their glory. There was the briefest sparkle of light before an immediate power cut plunged not only their house but the entire street into darkness. Everybody rushed out of their homes to see if their neighbours were all right and ask what they thought the problem was. Joan peeked out from behind her curtains and was going to stay put, until she realized that might look suspicious so rushed out of her front door with her best acting: 'Oh my, what could have happened? What a very strange thing to have occurred!'

Everyone on the street started screaming and pointing at her. Joan was horrified, thinking that her reputation must now be so bad she was perceived as some kind of local monster. What she didn't realize was that she had run out in her nightdress and open dressing gown, and the dressing gown cord had caught on fire (in her peeking she had stood too close to a candle). The only thing Joan knew was that Nellie had randomly drenched her in water from her front garden hose and she had absolutely no idea why she would do such a thing! 'You were on fire, Joan!' explained Nellie. 'Actually about to be fully on fire.'

Everybody started laughing (through relief, not necessarily unkindness, though of course Joan by now misconstrued that too). Next she saw Nellie waving frantically at her. 'Cover yourself,' she mouthed. It turned out that the bright moon was shining at the perfect angle to make Joan's dripping-wet nightdress appear, well, basically, let's not beat about the bush – it was completely see-through. Dearest Joan. Things really weren't going her way.

'Joan, I think you'd better go in and continue your saucy shenanigans in private,' teased Nellie, pointing at her nightdress. Joan looked down, screeched and jumped inside, slamming her door. She turned around to see Jessie on her back, paws in the air, writhing in hysterical giggles. Joan didn't blame her and as she squelched upstairs to dry off, she thought she might just have to find a way to give in to these recurring mishaps. Despite the bright moon, Joan, now in cosy pyjamas, gathered some more candles while they remained plunged in darkness. She made a clearing in the middle of the sitting room among the trees and lit (at a safe distance) some candles for Jessie to curl up next to. It felt like they were camping in the middle of a forest. It was beautiful. Joan crept to the kitchen to get some snacks and they feasted around their candles, which they called their campfire, even cooking some marshmallows. Joan, despite all, fell asleep with a big smile on her face, feeling as she used to on her youthful adventures.

The next morning, in the stark light of day, Joan's smile immediately fell away. This is when, I'm afraid, things were absolutely not even remotely fun or cosy. Quite the opposite. Joan gasped in horror, which woke Jessie up from a deep, dreaming sleep about chasing squirrels.

'Oh no, no, no!' wailed Joan. 'Jessie, look. Oh no!'

Their beloved trees had turned quite brown and were assuredly withering. Joan had been so excited about redecorating them that she hadn't noticed how unwell they had started looking and how many needles they had been shedding. Jessie shivered at the thought. She never moulted and couldn't imagine what it must be like to lose any fur. Or fir in this case. Joan could now see clearly how weak, dry and brittle the trees had become. Was she having to face the fact that her trees were dying? They had all been out of water for a very long time. In her desperation to stop them being stolen, and her love of having them to stay, Joan had become too preoccupied to consider practicalities. There were a few times when Jessie was going to tell her that she wasn't sure trees without roots could survive, but she was swept up in Joan's infectious joy with her latest enterprise. It had felt so long since she had seen her owner more like herself in that way. Could Joan get buckets of water to save them? Should she get new soil and big pots? What if they grew and started hitting the ceiling or knocking each other over as they widened? An indoor forest wasn't possible. This was a terrible pickle. A prickly pickle in fact. She didn't know what to do. You could say she couldn't see the wood for the trees . . .

Joan suddenly thought of Poodle Tree and how weak she too must be feeling – it was awful not knowing where her friend might have been taken. Jessie could see Joan looking very worried and came up with an idea. She put her paws on Joan's legs (which she isn't allowed to do so Joan knew it was urgent) and barked, 'Let's go and ask Sycamore.'

'Good idea, I need to be around somebody with real wisdom . . . Not that you aren't wise, Jessie . . .'

'Oh, don't worry, I know I'm wise. Who was it who had the idea to speak to Sycamore? Me, it was me. Let's go . . .'

Jessie felt immensely proud of herself and trotted off with her best little trot, head held high, imagining she was Best in Show at Crufts.

In no time at all, Joan leant against Sycamore and let out a slow breath. She could feel the soothing support of his trunk already. 'Hello, Sycamore.'

'Hello, my loves,' replied Sycamore, in his deep, calm voice.

'We are in a bit of a pickle, Sycamore.' Joan explained the situation. 'What can I do with my trees? Can they survive?'

'I would love to help you, Joan,' said Sycamore, 'but I am afraid I only have bad news. Those trees won't survive without water and nourishment from rich soil. Trees need roots and need to be planted. Many people don't know this, but we connect to each other via our roots, deep under the earth. We send each other messages and help one another. I am linked to not only other sycamore cousins in these streets, but other species too – I can feel that ash over there, she's had a hard day. There's a whole network of support we give to one another.'

'I had no idea, but that makes perfect sense. I suppose we all need to be connected?' Joan asked wistfully.

'I believe so,' said Sycamore. 'We trees never let one of our own suffer if we can help.'

'You really are the wisest and cleverest of all, Sycamore,' said Jessie. 'Even more than me, and that's saying something because I am very, very wise and clever.' She added pointedly to Joan, 'I mean, the other day I picked up a small ball, then threw it out of my mouth, and then ran after it. I was basically playing catch on my own. I rest my case.'

'You really don't have any answers for my trees, Sycamore?' asked Joan one last time in hope.

'I am afraid that I do not . . . umm . . . Hang on . . .' Sycamore stopped. 'Can you hear that?'

Joan couldn't hear anything and neither could Jessie, which was unusual for a dog if there was any kind of nearby sound. Jessie was particularly good at hearing ice-cream vans from miles away. But Sycamore, because of his root depth below the ground, could sense many sounds by vibration. And sure enough – after a couple of minutes, Jessie and then Joan were able to hear it too. The familiar *thud, thud* of the music from the men in their truck.

'It's the Christmas tree thieves,' said Sycamore. 'They're coming. I saw them two days ago and I heard them say that they might do one last scout around, as people coming back from winter holidays sometimes throw their trees out quite late in January.'

'This is it. I must rescue Poodle Tree. But how, Sycamore, how can we?' Joan implored.

'There is only one thing to do. You must get in your car and follow them.'

'Follow them?' said Joan and Jessie in unison, looking up at Sycamore a smidgeon nervously.

'You need to find out what they have actually been doing. Where they have been taking the trees. If you can't find a way to save your trees at home, perhaps next year you can make sure the January trees will be saved from these people. Now, hurry.'

They gave Sycamore a quick hug and rushed off.

Joan had never been in a car chase before. But with her renewed vigour, she was up for the challenge. She knew now she couldn't let the recent mishaps stop her from helping.

Joan got in her car and Jessie leapt up into the passenger seat, front paws just reaching to the dashboard so she could see. Slowly, they started to drive around looking for the truck. All of a sudden Jessie barked. There were the bearded men, parked outside a café, getting some sandwiches. Joan pulled in to watch.

'This feels like a stakeout,' said Joan.

'Where's the steak?' barked Jessie. 'Where is it?'

'No, I said stake*out* . . .'

'Where's the steak out of? I want the steak . . .'

'Stop thinking of steak – I said stakeout, like a police stakeout, a lookout . . .'

'Oh, that's very disappointing,' whined Jessie. 'Now all I can think about is steak.'

'Focus, Jessie!'

And indeed, they had to abruptly focus because the men were coming out of the café. Of course, yet again, at precisely the wrong moment, Daniel happened to walk past. He waved to Joan. Joan ducked. Not because of Daniel, but because she couldn't let the men heading back to their truck see her. Sadly, Daniel thought she was avoiding him and rushed on. Joan, focusing solely on the truck, missed Daniel's upset reaction entirely. Poor Daniel. He really was a rather unusually sweet man. But there's no time for me to tell you more about Daniel because the truck started moving off. As did Joan.

But then it stopped again! As did Joan. Now what were they doing?

On the pavement were two trees, dumped outside with all their decorations still on. Despite the cheerful tinsel wrapped around their branches, they looked nothing but mournful. Joan saw the men shove the trees unthinkingly into their truck, just like before. She couldn't believe that *still* no one saw these men like she did. No one else noticed that they weren't the usual rubbish clearers or gardeners. No one else seemed to care. But before Joan could contemplate this any further, the chase was on. The truck was speeding off. Right, it was time to find out where these mean, bearded men were taking her beloved January trees.

Joan knew she would have to drive a lot faster than normal to keep up with their truck, but she didn't realize quite how fast they would drive. This bad behaviour only convinced her further that they were doing something wrong. The men turned onto the main road and then immediately did a U-turn, which was illegal. In fact, they did the U-turn right in front of the 'No U-turns' sign!

Jessie shouted at Joan, 'Just turn – it's more important we chase them!' Joan performed a frighteningly swift U-turn, which also meant a U-turn for Jessie, who was flung from the passenger seat straight onto Joan's lap.

'Get off my lap, Jessie, I can't concentrate and I am nearly losing them already.'

'I got flung here. I have no intention of being here, thank you very much. When you take a left turn I will use the motion to swing myself back to the passenger seat.'

The first turn they had to take was not left but right, and to keep up with the truck they needed to take the corner at speed. This flung Jessie into the well of the driver's seat among the pedals.

'Oh my word!' shrieked Jessie. 'Don't stomp your smelly feet on me – I'm too pretty to be stomped on.'

'More to the point, don't get in the way of the brake pedal!'

'Which is the brake pedal? Help!' cried Jessie. (Jessie did get stuck in front of the brake pedal for a moment, but that worked out as it forced Joan to continue through an amber, nearly red, light. She was keeping up with the truck, if not entirely by choice.)

Luckily, they came to some traffic, which gave Joan a chance to grab Jessie and put her back on the passenger seat. They took a breath. Then they were off again, speeding down a busy high street. Joan had to drive so fast to keep up with the truck that she swerved to avoid a cyclist, nearly knocking over a fruit and vegetable stall which wobbled so violently that all the oranges and grapefruits rolled into the road, causing total chaos behind her. Joan looked in the mirror to see what was happening but then nearly hit a pedestrian crossing the road and swerved again, this time onto the pavement, where some material from a curtain shop got caught in her car window and draped itself across the windscreen. Jessie and Joan started really screaming as now they couldn't see anything.

'Windscreen wipers – QUICK!' yelled Jessie. Joan put them on fast speed and thankfully the material swept off just in time for her to put the brake on for a momentary emergency stop – they were inches away from driving straight into the truck itself. Golly gosh! To put it mildly. Thankfully Joan and Jessie had managed not to injure anyone – in fact, the material that had whooshed off the car landed around a woman's neck, and she seemed rather pleased to suddenly have a pashmina about her person, and a group of children had enjoyed using the grapefruits like roller skates – but this really was becoming quite the terrifying chase. Joan was determined not to give up. They turned sharply and they were off again, this time heading onto the motorway and out of the city.

'I wonder where we will end up,' said Jessie. 'Oooh, maybe we will go to that park with the big pond and I can chase the ducks and eat all the swan poo.'

'This is not about you going on a walk,' said Joan swerving into the fast lane.

'Yes, quite, got distracted thinking about swan poo.'

'You're disgusting. Now, will you focus?! This is the most serious mission we have ever been on.'

Jessie started making a strange noise that sounded like a cross between a whine and a howl, as their pace quickened.

'Now what are you doing?' asked Joan.

'Making a police siren noise – it will help us feel powerful and keep going.'

'Nee naw, nee naw, nee naw,' shouted Jessie and Joan, speeding past cars on the motorway.

Then the truck started crossing lanes, making for a junction turn-off. Joan had to keep her wits about her to do the same. She got shouted at by a lorry driver that she swept in front of, but apart from that she got off the motorway safely, still following the truck.

It always amazed Joan how quickly you could leave a town or city for rolling countryside. They were now on a straight stretch of road surrounded by nothing but grassy fields, albeit still busy with rushing cars and vans.

'Quick, turn! They've turned off!' noticed Jessie.

Joan bravely took the unexpected turning, the tyres on her small car screeching as she and Jessie screeched too. It was a turning that was hard to see, especially for people going at the speed they normally do dashing from A to B (we must miss so much preciousness by rushing in life, don't you think?). But by taking it (albeit not by choice in this situation), they found themselves on a lane with stunning hedgerows, the beautiful song of a winter robin and a fancy flock of blue tits. Just the kind of thing Joan and Jessie love and are always grateful for.

But now was not the time to calmly stop and drink it all in. Although they were slowing down. Because the truck was. Which was odd because there were no other turnings coming up.

'Oh no, they've seen us – they must know we have been following them,' realized Joan.

'Oh help, what should we do?' Jessie trembled.

'Let's stop and pretend to be asleep,' said Joan. It was the only thing she could think of in the heat of the moment.

'Oh help, oh help, oh help,' Jessie frantically muttered to herself as she curled up on the seat, trying to pretend to sleep with her heart racing faster than when she chased ducks into a pond.

The men got out of their truck and approached Joan and Jessie's car. One of them knocked on the window. Joan and Jessie continued to pretend to be asleep, hoping they would go away.

But he knocked louder. Joan, employing her best acting again, wound down the window, yawned and said blurrily, 'Oh, hello, sorry, I was asleep, having a nap in the car.'

'Really?' said the man incredulously.

Joan felt scared and Jessie started shaking.

'Yes,' said Joan. 'Just a little sleep.'

'Well, that seems very odd because you were following us, driving right behind us, and then, what, you suddenly fell asleep? At the wheel? In the middle of the road?'

'Umm . . . well . . . umm . . .' Joan's mind froze as to how to justify her story. The other man had approached by now.

'Apparently they were asleep and not following us, ha ha,' said the man to his friend.

Looking closely at the second man, Jessie sat bolt upright and stared at him with wide eyes. Joan was staring too.

'Hang on, where's your beard?' asked Joan.

The strangest thing was going on. The second man who had just got out of the truck no longer had a beard but was clean-shaven and looked completely different.

'Oh, umm . . . well . . .' It was his turn not to know what to say.

Joan also noticed that his boiler suit had been removed to reveal a smart green tracksuit upon his long lean frame. She then looked more carefully at the first man, who was smaller and portlier and leaning into her car window (with not the freshest of breath, but that wasn't as important right now). She peered at his beard up close. And guess what? It was fake. She noticed the elastic bands around his ears holding it on. 'You're wearing a fake beard? Why have you got a fake beard on?' asked Joan, who then, without thinking, pulled the beard towards her and pinged it back onto his face.

'Ow!' said the man.

Joan took a deep breath, summoned as much courage as she had, got out of her car and said in her sternest voice, 'Now, look here, you are both clearly up to something: you drive very dangerously, you steal Christmas trees, you are in disguise, and now I have caught you and I will report you. I have your registration number so there's no getting away now – you might as well tell me everything or else.'

If Jessie had been able to clap with her front paws, she would have done so.

The first man took off his beard. Joan and Jessie stared again. He seemed so different without it. Both men took their caps off and Joan could see their shiny blue eyes. They each looked surprisingly kind, and if they had any lines on their faces, they were smile lines, not frowns. But Joan and Jessie weren't going to fall for anything.

'I suppose we'd better explain,' said the first man.

'I suppose you very much better had.' Joan was still emboldened.

'It's probably better to show you rather than tell you. Follow us, it's not much further to go.' And with that, they got back into their truck.

Joan and Jessie looked at each other. They knew they were thinking the same thing – this was a risk. They had no idea what they might see or face, whether they might end up being taken away in the truck too (oh gosh, what an awful thought, I am so sorry). Or they could keep following and trust that they might get an answer. They had come this far . . . They decided to brave it. And so they set off, singing their usual tune to stop themselves feeling afraid: 'Off to embrace a mission, a wonderful J and J mission . . .'

The men took them a little further down the country road before turning into a gravel lane. This was scary for Joan and Jessie, as no one would find them here, but just as they were thinking the worst, they turned a corner and saw the most amazing and surprising sight you could ever imagine.

I wonder what you are thinking it might be? I won't keep you in suspense.

Joan parked the car, and from the top of the hill they were on, she and Jessie found themselves gazing out over the most beautiful forest they had ever seen. Not just any forest, but a forest of pine trees. And not just any normal forest of pine trees but a forest of pine trees with stars and angels at the top of them. Yes, that's right, Christmas trees. These trees looked so dazzling, their thick green needles shimmering in the low winter sunset, sparkling naturally without the need of tinsel. Not only did these trees, in the wild, all have angels and stars (and a cowboy hat) at the top of them, but (and you might not believe this) they were dancing! Rows and rows of Christmas trees in fields as far as the eye could see, some dancing in pairs, some line dancing in a row, some doing a conga. Joan and Jessie could hear them all whooping and cheering. These Christmas trees were clearly more than happy, growing and healthy, all connected to each other.

'Bet you weren't expecting that, were you?' said one of the men.

Joan and Jessie just shook their heads, unable to either speak or bark. They couldn't believe what they were witnessing. Eventually Joan turned back to the men. 'But . . . hang on . . .' She stumbled on her words as the other man had also taken his boiler suit off and they were both standing in matching green outfits, with similar thick, clean auburn and strawberry blond hair (almost shining).

Jessie wondered if they were angels (such were their kindly rosy faces, the type you feel instantly at home and comfortable with), but if anything, she thought, they themselves looked a bit like dancing Christmas trees. One small and bushy, the other tall and straggly. Joan recovered herself. 'So, you were taking the trees here all this time?'

'Yes,' said the men.

'You were saving them?'

'Yes.'

'We thought you were stealing them, or selling them off . . . or . . . I don't understand,' said Joan. The men introduced themselves as Dudley and Cliff and explained it all.

It turned out that Dudley and Cliff were very like Joan. They loved nature and couldn't bear to see the trees discarded on the streets after Christmas. They knew that the January Christmas trees would be thrown away, either as food for animals in zoos or put into a wood chipper to be sold as chippings. Dudley and Cliff knew these weren't necessarily terrible things in themselves, but they didn't believe it should be the fate of most trees, which deserved to be restored to their natural glory. For the past few years, they had picked up the trees off streets in January and replanted them. They put a star on top of each tree to acknowledge the gift and service it had given, and then they left them to grow. Dudley and Cliff had created an amazing woodland, giving the trees their life back. And so the trees danced with joy.

Joan had two burning questions. You likely have the same ones. I certainly do.

'But how come you disguised yourselves – the beards, the caps, the thumping music, tossing the trees neglectfully into your truck?'

'Because that way we fitted in and didn't get noticed,' began Cliff.

'What do you mean?' asked Joan, confused.

'It's sad to say,' continued Dudley, 'but the way we avoid being caught by the rubbish clearers is to behave how they do in January. Well, how many people do in January. Burdened, back to a sense of toil, smiles hidden (hence covering ours with beards). It's as if the love and jollity of Christmas are discarded along with the trees.'

'Oh my goodness, I have had the exact same thoughts.'

'It's other kinds of people that stick out.'

'I think I stick out,' said Joan.

'Exactly,' the men said.

'What do you mean?' Joan was desperately trying to keep up. Jessie was hoping they weren't going to be rude about her beloved owner. It was only for Jessie to say that Joan had smelly feet and farted when she went up the stairs.

'You are a good and fun person, you care, you smile and chat to people, you make a difference, so people notice you,' explained Cliff generously.

Jessie snuggled up to Joan's legs and sat on her feet, knowing this was absolutely true. She was very proud to belong to her.

'You could tell that it looked like we were doing something wrong. You noticed the trees and worried about them. You know when something's not right, and you try to make your part of the world better.' Joan remembered an old saying of her mother's: *It's always right for you to do the right thing, even if people get the wrong idea about you.*

Before Joan could dwell on the perceptiveness of her dearest mother, she had a truly awful thought. 'Oh no, the trees in my house!' she exclaimed. 'I saved thirty-three trees, or I thought I was saving thirty-three trees from you, and now they are dying. I killed all those trees when they could have been replanted here. Oh no . . .'

Joan thought she was going to cry, but Dudley gently put his hand on her shoulder. 'Don't worry, it shouldn't be too late. We'll bring them here.'

And then came the next burning question.

'Hang on,' she said. 'How do they survive? My sycamore friend told me it would be impossible if they'd been chopped down.'

Dudley and Cliff looked at each other. They were feeling a bit shy, but they felt they could trust Joan with their secret. It turned out that Dudley and Cliff didn't know if any of the trees without roots would survive when they first brought them here.

But when the tree trunks touched the beautiful, rich soil on this part of the planet, a miracle happened. Their roots started growing back as if they were being pulled down into the very ground the trees needed to belong.

'They just started growing roots again? Before your very eyes?' exclaimed Joan, her own eyes wide in amazement.

'Yes.'

Joan and Jessie were now not only wide-eyed but wide-mouthed. Jessie didn't even notice when a fly flew into hers.

'We think it's because we naturally flourish when we're planted in the right place. In the right soil,' said Cliff.

'I believe nothing is impossible,' added Dudley. 'Although, it often feels impossible to believe that!'

Perhaps there are always two aspects to life – the ordinary, everyday actions we need and have to do, and then the 'extraordinary ordinary', available to those who dare to believe and look for it. Where you might find miracles small and big, explicable and inexplicable. Back to life's mysteries, eh?

'What might be possible for my trees at home? What do I need to do?'

'You go out for the night, and we will do it for you.'

'Out for the night?' repeated Joan, staring at Dudley and Cliff as if they had said the most shocking thing yet. In many ways they had – a fifty-five-year-old woman had likely put her going-out days behind her and considered taking the bins out late enough of a thrill. Jessie put her head to one side, looking confused too. Joan continued, 'I haven't been out for the night in . . . well . . . I don't go anywhere much any more . . .'

'Perhaps this is your chance to change that,' Cliff replied softly.

Suddenly, Joan and Jessie heard a familiar voice. 'Hello, is that you? Joan? Jessie? Hello?!'

They followed the voice and then, they saw her. You couldn't mistake that tree shape anywhere – it was Poodle Tree! She was planted on the edge of the forest and was dancing with another tree her size.

Joan and Jessie raced down the hill to their friend. 'Hello! Hurray, you are saved!'

'Isn't it wonderful?!' said Poodle Tree. 'Thank you for looking after me and my friends . . . I hope you are okay. I am so sor— Ooops, I nearly said "sorry"!'

'Well done,' said Joan, 'because I am very okay and in fact so grateful I tripped over you that day.'

'And I am so grateful to have met you. You gave me hope. Although I couldn't have hoped for anything as amazing as this. Isn't it extraordinary here? All of us trees have had a second chance at life when we thought our lives were over. We can't stop dancing.'

Poodle Tree didn't realize it, but what she said gave Joan an idea – one that ended up changing her life.

So here we are, towards the end of our tale. I can share with you that as Dudley and Cliff removed the thirty-three trees from Joan's house, Joan chose to go to the local dance club in the church hall. She hadn't danced for so many years and crept in rather shyly, holding Jessie for comfort. The first person she saw was Daniel. Yes, the very same Daniel who ran the dry cleaner's and tailor's, who always bumped into Joan in her most embarrassing moments. Joan had an anxious wobble and nearly ran out, thinking that his presence must mean she was going to make a colossal fool of herself. She wasn't sure she had the nerve for another mishap or muddle, despite feeling like she was doing the right thing for herself.

Daniel was sitting alone on a chair watching the dancing, and before Joan could escape, he turned to see her. He looked shocked and then stood up. Joan put Jessie on a chair – Jessie sat there watching eagerly to see what was going to happen.

'Hello, Joan,' said Daniel. 'Haven't seen you in here before.'

'Hello, Daniel. No, I haven't been dancing for years. Do you dance?'

'Yes, I love it, though often I just watch because there isn't a partner I love to dance with.'

'That's why I stopped,' said Joan, feeling a brief pang of sadness having not seen her friends from those dancing days in so long.

'Don't suppose . . . no . . . of course not.'

'I would love to,' said Joan.

'What?'

'Were you about to ask me to dance? Oh, maybe you weren't. I know you think I am odd,' muttered Joan.

'I was going to ask you to dance,' said Daniel.

'You were?'

'Yes. I don't think you're odd. I think you're wonderful!'

She smiled, took the compliment in – it made her feel vibrant and beautiful. 'Thank you.' Joan realized that recent events had meant she had become unusually down on herself. She'd lost herself a little. She took a deep breath, 'I would love to dance with you, Daniel.'

'Just as dance partners, of course – your boyfriend doesn't need to be concerned.'

'Yes, just as dance partners. Although I don't have a boyfriend. Much of what you think, I suspect, is not true,' said Joan as they walked onto the dance floor.

Joan and Daniel started dancing together, so naturally, immediately falling into a perfect rhythm. The familiar movement almost instantly created a sense of freedom in Joan's body and spirit – she felt twenty-five again!

Jessie lay down on the chair, in nothing but awe at her owner – no need to put a paw over her face this time.

And now, we are right at the end of our tale.

I must say goodbye. Or, hopefully, au revoir, as I tell you that as Poodle Tree and all her Christmas tree friends danced the night away under the stars, and as Dudley and Cliff planted Joan's trees to join them in the forest, Joan and Daniel danced joyfully all evening. They twirled and swirled, smiling, laughing, completely comfortable in each other's arms.

It felt exactly like what Poodle Tree had said to Joan.

She was getting a second chance at life.

The End

PENGUIN MICHAEL JOSEPH

UK | USA | Canada | Ireland | Australia
India | New Zealand | South Africa

Penguin Michael Joseph is part of the Penguin Random House group of companies
whose addresses can be found at global.penguinrandomhouse.com

Penguin Random House UK
One Embassy Gardens, 8 Viaduct Gardens, London SW11 7BW

penguin.co.uk

First published 2025
004

Penguin
Random House
UK

Set in Recoleta Alt and Sabon LT Pro
Colour origination by Altaimage, London
Printed and bound in Great Britain by Bell and Bain Ltd, Glasgow

The authorized representative in the EEA is Penguin Random House Ireland,
Morrison Chambers, 32 Nassau Street, Dublin D02 YH68

A CIP catalogue record for this book is available from the British Library

ISBN: 978–0–241–79629–0

Penguin Random House is committed to a sustainable future
for our business, our readers and our planet. This book is made from
Forest Stewardship Council® certified paper